NATURE'S
CREEPIEST
CREATURES

# CREEPY BUGS

By Nicole Shea

Gareth Stevens
Publishing

**Please visit our website, www.garethstevens.com. For a free color catalog of all our high-quality books, call toll free 1-800-542-2595 or fax 1-877-542-2596.**

**Library of Congress Cataloging-in-Publication Data**

Shea, Nicole, 1976-
Creepy bugs / Nicole Shea.
    p. cm. — (Nature's creepiest creatures)
Includes index.
ISBN 978-1-4339-6491-6 (pbk.)
ISBN 978-1-4339-6492-3 (6-pack)
ISBN 978-1-4339-6489-3 (library binding)
1. Insects—Juvenile literature. 2. Arthropoda—Juvenile literature.  I. Title.
QL467.2.S516 2012
595.7—dc23

2011029447

First Edition

Published in 2012 by
**Gareth Stevens Publishing**
111 East 14th Street, Suite 349
New York, NY 10003

Copyright © 2012 Gareth Stevens Publishing

Designer: Haley W. Harasymiw
Editor: Kristen Rajczak

Photo credits: Cover, p. 1 Hein von Horsten/Getty Images; pp. 4, 5, 6, 7, 10, 11, 12, 13, 15, 18, 19, 20, 21 (dung beetle) Shutterstock.com; p. 9 Randy Peralta/Flickr/Getty Images; p. 17 Visuals Unlimited/Getty Images; p. 21 (froghopper) courtesy of Wikipedia Commons.

Printed in the United States of America

CPSIA compliance information: Batch #CW12GS: For further information contact Gareth Stevens, New York, New York at 1-800-542-2595.

# CONTENTS

Words in the glossary appear in **bold** type the first time they are used in the text.

# THE WORLD OF BUGS

There are about 1 million known kinds of bugs in the world! Bugs live everywhere, and for their size, they're the world-record holders for just about anything you can think of. They can jump the farthest, lift the most, and go without food the longest. They're also a very important part of the world around us.

While some bugs, like ants and bees, are very familiar to us, many more look and act stranger than any movie creature!

flea

## FREAKY FACT:

Fleas can jump 200 times their length. This means they have no trouble jumping off your pet and onto the couch!

The rhinoceros beetle can carry more than 800 times its own weight.

5

# WHAT'S A BUG?

The word "bug" usually means an insect. Insects are small animals with six legs and an **exoskeleton** made from a hard matter called chitin. They have a body divided into a head, **thorax**, and **abdomen**.

The American cockroach is one common—and often unwelcome—insect in the United States. Cockroaches like warm, dark places like basements. These bugs creep out at night to eat bread, fruit, dead bugs, old rice, cloth, and hair!

cockroach

## FREAKY FACT:

A cockroach can live for about a week after its head has been removed!

The most common cockroaches in the United States are the German, American, and brown-banded cockroaches.

# A CREEPY NEST FOR A GROWING FAMILY

Have you ever seen a beehive? Bees and other bugs build nests to keep their eggs and **larvae** safe while they grow. However, some bugs' nests are creepier than others.

A mother spider wasp has a scary way of preparing a nest for her young. She attacks and **paralyzes** a spider. Then, she brings it back to a little nest she's made in soil or rotting wood. She lays an egg on the spider, which is still alive. When the larva hatches, it eats the spider!

## FREAKY FACT:

If the spider is very large, the egg laid by the spider wasp will become a female. If the spider is small, the egg will become a male.

This spider wasp is paralyzing a spider to take back to her nest.

9

# PRAYING MANTIS

A praying mantis, or mantid, hides in plain sight. These bugs are green or brown and look like a leaf or branch. This **camouflage** helps them escape danger and catch **prey**.

The praying mantis has an alien-looking head that seems to turn almost completely around. It stays very still with its front legs held up like it's praying. When a praying mantis spots its dinner, it moves faster than we can see! The spikes on its legs keep its meal from getting away.

praying mantis

## FREAKY FACT:

Sometimes a female mantis bites off the male's head after **mating**.

Baby praying mantises, called nymphs, often eat each other.

# CREEPY HELPERS

The house centipede has 15 pairs of legs! The last pair is almost twice as long as the centipede's entire body. All these legs help the centipedes move quickly across floors and walls. House centipedes may look scary, but they help get rid of other common household pests such as cockroaches and ants.

There are many kinds of centipedes. They may have as many as 177 pairs of legs! Soil centipedes are the creepiest of the bunch, though. They can be up to a foot (30 cm) long and can live for 10 years!

garden centipede

## FREAKY FACT:

Centipedes can regrow a leg if they lose one.

Centipedes can use their legs to attack more than one insect at a time.

13

# SUN SPIDERS

Sun spiders aren't true spiders. But at about 6 inches (15.2 cm) long, these hairy bugs can be as creepy as tarantulas! They're sometimes called wind scorpions because they're fast runners and look like scorpions. Sun spiders are also called camel spiders.

Sun spiders commonly live in the desert. They like to hunt at night. Sun spiders catch insects and even small lizards with their strong arms. They may eat so much that they're unable to move afterwards!

## FREAKY FACT:

Some sun spiders have powerful jaws that are up to 1/3 the length of their body.

Sun spiders can run as fast as 10 miles (16 km) per hour!

15

# BOMBS AWAY!

Some bugs scare off **predators** by biting or stinging. Others just fly away.

Bombardier beetles can't instantly take flight. Their wings have covers and don't come out fast enough for the beetle to escape by flying. However, they have an unusual way to keep from being dinner. A bombardier beetle stores special **chemicals** inside its body. When it's in danger, it combines them. The chemicals become boiling hot and toxic as they mix. Then they explode from the tip of the beetle's abdomen with a loud pop!

## FREAKY FACT:

The bombardier beetle's chemical spray doesn't kill a predator, but it does burn and stain skin.

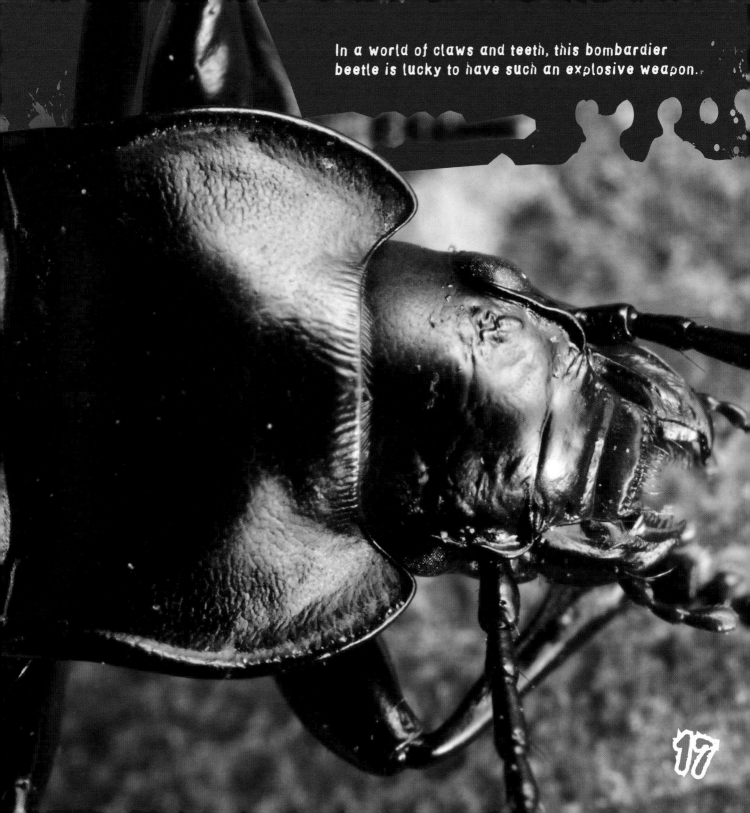

In a world of claws and teeth, this bombardier beetle is lucky to have such an explosive weapon.

17

# DINNER

You name it, bugs eat it. Many bugs eat plants or waste. Bugs even eat other bugs.

Some kinds of assassin bugs have a freaky way of doing this. Since many bugs have a hard exoskeleton that's tough to eat, an assassin bug squirts a liquid into its prey. It turns the prey's insides into mush! Then, the assassin bug uses its special mouth to suck the mush out. Some assassin bugs just drink plant juices, though.

assassin bug

## FREAKY FACT:

One kind of assassin bug is called the kissing bug because it often bites people near their mouth as they sleep.

An assassin bug gets its name from the word "assassin," which means "killer."

19

# TWO MILLION STRONG

Bugs may live in large groups called **colonies**. Some army ants live in colonies of 2 million or more members. A huge group of ants moving through the jungle looks really creepy!

Instead of building a nest, army ants form one with their own bodies. They use little hooks on their legs to hang together. Army ants catch and kill prey much bigger than themselves as a group, too. The weirdest part? Army ants are blind!

army ant colony

## FREAKY FACT:

Army ant colonies are so huge that you can actually hear them marching through the forest.

# RECORD-BREAKING BUGS

| RECORD | BUG |
|---|---|
| longest | A stick insect that was 22 inches (56 cm) long was found in 2008. |
| smallest | It would take 200 fairyflies laid end to end to equal 1 inch (2.5 cm). |
| strongest | A dung beetle lifted 1,141 times its own weight in 2010. |
| fastest | Dragonflies can fly 35 miles (56 km) per hour. |
| shortest life | Adult mayflies live 1 day. |
| highest jumper | Froghoppers have jumped 28 inches (70 cm) into the air. |

froghopper

# GLOSSARY

**abdomen:** the section of an insect's body that contains the stomach

**camouflage:** colors or shapes that allow an animal to hide in its surroundings

**chemical:** a matter or liquid that when mixed with something causes a change

**colony:** a group of animals living and working together

**exoskeleton:** the hard outer covering of an animal's body

**larvae:** young insects that have a worm-like form. The singular form is "larva."

**mate:** to come together to make babies

**paralyze:** to make unable to move

**predator:** an animal that hunts other animals for food

**prey:** an animal that is hunted by other animals for food

**thorax:** the section of an insect's body that contains the heart and lungs

# For More Information

## Books

O'Neill, Amanda. *I Wonder Why Spiders Spin Webs and Other Questions About Creepy Crawlies.* New York, NY: Kingfisher, 2011.

Parker, Steve. *100 Things You Should Know About Bugs.* Broomall, PA: Mason Crest Publishers, 2011.

## Websites

**Going Bug-gy! Facts and Fun About Insects**
*teacher.scholastic.com/activities/bugs/*
Play games to learn more about insects.

**National Geo Wild: Bugs**
*animals.nationalgeographic.com/animals/bugs/*
Read about many other insects and see their pictures.

# INDEX